MALEKITH AND HIS ALLIES ARE WAGING WAR ACROSS THE TEN REALMS. TO STOP HIM, VOLSTAGG PICKED UP THE HAMMER OF THE ULTIMATE THOR AND BECAME THE WAR THOR — BUT ITS POWER DROVE HIM INTO A MAD BLOODLUST. THOR COULD NOT CALM HIM, BUT JANE FOSTER REMINDED HIM OF HIS HUMANITY, AND HE GAVE UP THE HAMMER.

AND SO THE WAR — AGAINST MALEKITH AND AGAINST JANE'S CANCER — CONTINUES. SO, TOO, DOES THE LEGACY OF THOR AND OF THE ODINSON WHO HAS LONG CARRIED THAT NAME. THIS IS A STORY OF THE ANCIENT, THE PRESENT AND THE FORETOLD…

DEDICATED TO MICHAEL W. WILSON

THOR CREATED BY **STAN LEE, LARRY LIEBER** & **JACK KIRBY**

COLLECTION EDITOR: **JENNIFER GRÜNWALD**
ASSISTANT EDITOR: **CAITLIN O'CONNELL**
ASSOCIATE MANAGING EDITOR: **KATERI WOODY**
EDITOR, SPECIAL PROJECTS: **MARK D. BEAZLEY**

VP PRODUCTION & SPECIAL PROJECTS: **JEFF YOUNGQUIST**
SVP PRINT, SALES & MARKETING: **DAVID GABRIEL**
BOOK DESIGNER: **ADAM DEL RE**

EDITOR IN CHIEF: **C.B. CEBULSKI**
CHIEF CREATIVE OFFICER: **JOE QUESADA**
PRESIDENT: **DAN BUCKLEY**
EXECUTIVE PRODUCER: **ALAN FINE**

MIGHTY THOR VOL. 5: THE DEATH OF THE MIGHTY THOR. Contains material originally published in magazine form as MIGHTY THOR #700-706 and MIGHTY THOR: AT THE GATES OF VALHALLA #1. First printing 2018. ISBN 978-1-302-90661-0. Published by MARVEL WORLDWIDE, INC., a subsidiary of MARVEL ENTERTAINMENT, LLC. OFFICE OF PUBLICATION: 135 West 50th Street, New York, NY 10020. Copyright © 2018 MARVEL No similarity between any of the names, characters, persons, and/or institutions in this magazine with those of any living or dead person or institution is intended, and any such similarity which may exist is purely coincidental. **Printed in Canada.** DAN BUCKLEY, President, Marvel Entertainment; JOHN NEE, Publisher; JOE QUESADA, Chief Creative Officer; TOM BREVOORT, SVP of Publishing; DAVID BOGART, SVP of Business Affairs & Operations, Publishing & Partnership; DAVID GABRIEL, SVP of Sales & Marketing, Publishing; JEFF YOUNGQUIST, VP of Production & Special Projects; DAN CARR, Executive Director of Publishing Technology; ALEX MORALES, Director of Publishing Operations; DAN EDINGTON, Managing Editor; SUSAN CRESPI, Production Manager; STAN LEE, Chairman Emeritus. For information regarding advertising in Marvel Comics or on Marvel.com, please contact Vit DeBellis, Custom Solutions & Integrated Advertising Manager, at vdebellis@marvel.com. For Marvel subscription inquiries, please call 888-511-5480. **Manufactured between 10/5/2018 and 11/6/2018 by SOLISCO PRINTERS, SCOTT, QC, CANADA.**

10 9 8 7 6 5 4 3 2 1

THE MIGHTY THOR

THE DEATH OF THE MIGHTY THOR

WRITER
JASON AARON

MIGHTY THOR #700

ARTISTS
WALTER SIMONSON & **MATTHEW WILSON**, **RUSSELL DAUTERMAN** & **WILSON**, **DANIEL ACUÑA**, **JAMES HARREN** & **DAVE STEWART**, **BECKY CLOONAN** & **STEWART**, **DAS PASTORAS**, **CHRIS BURNHAM** & **IVE SVORCINA**, **ANDREW MacLEAN** & **STEWART**, **JILL THOMPSON**, **MIKE DEL MUNDO** AND **OLIVIER COIPEL** & **STEWART**

MIGHTY THOR #701

ARTIST	COLOR ARTIST
JAMES HARREN	**DAVE STEWART**

MIGHTY THOR #702-706

ARTIST	COLOR ARTIST
RUSSELL DAUTERMAN	**MATTHEW WILSON**

MIGHTY THOR: AT THE GATES OF VALHALLA

ARTISTS	COLOR ARTIST
JEN BARTEL & **RAMÓN K. PÉREZ**	**MATTHEW WILSON**

COVER ART
RUSSELL DAUTERMAN & **MATTHEW WILSON** (#700-705),
RUSSELL DAUTERMAN (#706) AND **NICK DERINGTON** (AT THE GATES OF VALHALLA)

LETTERER	ASSOCIATE EDITOR	EDITOR
VC's JOE SABINO	**SARAH BRUNSTAD**	**WIL MOSS**

THE BLOOD OF THE NORNS

THE ODINSON.
THE UNWORTHY THOR.

KARNILLA.
QUEEN OF THE NORNS.

THIS IS ONE
OF THOSE.

BAOOOM

AND HERE I WAS HAVING SUCH A *LOVELY* MORNING.

"IT'S REALLY GOOD TO SEE YOU MAKE IT IN TODAY. WE WERE STARTING TO GET *WORRIED* ABOUT YOU."

EARLIER.

IT'S BEEN WAY TOO LONG SINCE YOUR LAST TREATMENT, *DR. FOSTER.*

YEAH, WELL, YOU KNOW. LIFE SOMETIMES GETS IN THE WAY.

AND SO DO SPACE GODS AND DARK ELVES AND WAR THORS.

WHILE JANE FOSTER SOARS ABOVE THE SPIRES OF MIDGARD, SOMEWHERE FAR ACROSS THE GALAXY *ANOTHER* THOR DEALS WITH BEING *GROUNDED*.

HE WAS CALLED THE *WAR THOR*, AND HIS THUNDER STRUCK TERROR ACROSS THE REALMS. BUT NOW HE IS ONCE AGAIN KNOWN ONLY AS...

VOLSTAGG... PLEASE BELIEVE US WHEN WE TELL YOU, THIS IS FOR YOUR OWN GOOD.

THE ODINSON TOLD US WHAT HAPPENED. HOW YOU... LOST YOUR MIND BECAUSE OF THAT OTHER HAMMER.

THE *THUNDER GUARD* JUST NEEDS TO PUT YOU SOMEWHERE SAFE SO THE HEALERS CAN EXAMINE YOU.

ARE THE BONDS REALLY NECESSARY? THIS IS *VOLSTAGG*. WE ALL KNOW HE WOULDN'T HURT A--

KRADDA

DOOM

OH, NO.

YOU ALL SHOULD *RUN* NOW.

NO, KEEP HIM AWAY FROM IT! *KEEP HIM BACK!*

IT CAME.

VOLSTAGG, NO! DON'T TOUCH IT!

IT CAME FOR *ME.*

ONLY WAY. TO STOP THE FIRE.

GAGH, CAN'T BUDGE HIM! HE'S TOO--

ONLY WAY TO END THE WAR.

VOLSTAGG! DON'T--

THERE ALWAYS HAS BEEN.

MIDGARD.
896 A.D.

NAY!

THEIR WARSHIPS ARE CUTTING RIGHT THROUGH US LIKE SURTUR'S FLAMING SWORD!

WE CANNOT STOP THEM! THERE...THERE ARE JUST TOO ODIN-DAMNED MANY!

AND PRAY FOR MORE TROLLS!

THERE ARE NOT ENOUGH!

YOUNG THOR.
GOD OF THE VIKINGS.

QUICKLY, BESEECH MY FATHER IN ASGARD!

NO THOR HAS EVER LOOKED FORWARD TO WAR. BUT THEY DO CRAVE COMBAT. AS A NEWBORN BABE CRAVES ITS MOTHER'S MILK.

THE WEAPONS HALL OF ASGARD.

HHRRRRGGGH!!!

BATTLE IS HOW THEY PROVE THEMSELVES. HOW THEY BECOME WHO IT IS THEY'RE MEANT TO BE. ONE MIGHT EVEN SAY...

...IT'S IN THEIR BLOOD.

AH, I DO SO ENJOY FAMILY REUNIONS.

YOU REMEMBER MY BELOVED SON, *FENRIS*, I ASSUME? I HAVE LOOSED HIM FROM GLEIPNIR, THOSE CRUEL CHAINS FORGED BY THE ALL-FATHER.

HE'S QUITE ANXIOUS TO GET REACQUAINTED WITH THE REST OF HIS KIN, ESPECIALLY HIS *LEGENDARY UNCLE*. AREN'T YOU, FENRIS?

ALL I SEE IS *MEAT*.

AND ALL I HEAR IS *BARKING*. TELL ME, LOKI...

...DOES YOUR DOG HAVE ANY *BITE*?

BATTLE AND THUNDER AND URU. THESE ARE THE THINGS THAT MAKE A THOR.

HRRRGGH! *MOVE*, YOU STUPID HAMMER!

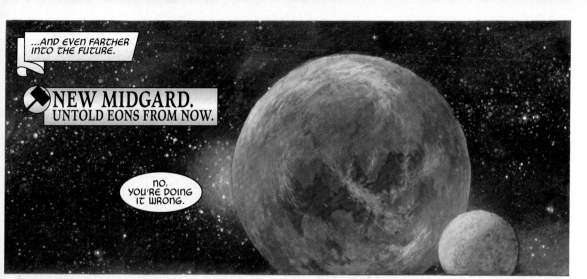

...AND EVEN FARTHER INTO THE FUTURE.

NEW MIDGARD.
UNTOLD EONS FROM NOW.

NO, YOU'RE DOING IT WRONG.

THIS ISN'T HOW THE ALL-GRANDFATHER SHOWED US. THIS ISN'T WHAT NEW MIDGARD NEEDS.

ELLISIV IS RIGHT. LESS THUNDER AND MORE RAIN, ATLI.

RAIN IS BORING, FRIGG. THUNDER ISN'T.

BUT THUNDER DOESN'T MAKE THE PLANTS GROW.

I'LL SHOW YOU THUNDER, SISTER!

KRAKOOOM

THEY'RE FIGHTING AGAIN.

ARE THE GODDESSES ANGRY BECAUSE WE DON'T WORSHIP THEM ENOUGH? IS THAT WHY THEY FIGHT?

THEY FIGHT BECAUSE THERE'S TOO DAMN MUCH OF THEIR GRANDFATHER IN THEM. TOO MUCH OF *ME.*

KING THOR.
ALL-FATHER AT THE END OF TIME.

AND I DIDN'T CREATE YOU SO YOU COULD WORSHIP US.

THEN WHY ARE WE HERE?

YOU HAVE NO IDEA HOW LONG MEN HAVE BEEN ASKING THAT QUESTION OF THEIR GODS.

AND DID THEIR GODS EVER ANSWER?

NOT TYPICALLY, NO. GODS COULD BE BASTARDS LIKE THAT.

BUT I WILL TELL YOU NOW, *JANE AND STEVE* OF NEW MIDGARD, WHAT THOSE OTHER GODS NEVER WOULD.

YOU ARE HERE TO *LIVE.*

TO GROW AND DREAM AND MAKE THIS WORLD YOUR HOME. AND TO FIND YOUR OWN WAY, YOUR OWN PLACE IN THE COSMOS, GODS BE DAMNED. MYSELF INCLUDED.

BUT THOR IS A *GOOD* GOD.

THOR IS A *TIRED* GOD.

STORY! STORY!

AH, BUT I SUPPOSE I DO HAVE TIME FOR JUST ONE MORE TALE.

HAVE I EVER TOLD YOU CHILDREN HOW I DEFEATED GALACTUS WITH JUST ONE ARM?

AND SO KING THOR TELLS THE STORY OF HOW HE SAVED THE EARTH FROM THE EATER OF WORLDS, USING THE WEAPON OF ONE OF HIS GREATEST ENEMIES.

THE WEAPON OF GORR THE GOD BUTCHER.

BUT WHAT KING THOR DOES NOT KNOW IS THAT THE STORY OF ALL-BLACK THE NECROSWORD DID NOT END.

THAT IT CONTINUES ON, ELSEWHERE AT THE END OF TIME, IN THE DEEPEST REACHES OF SPACE...

IN THE FORM OF BLACK GALACTUS, THE BUTCHER OF WORLDS.

ALL WORLDS MUST DIE!

THE NECROSWORD HAD NOT BEEN DESTROYED, BUT INSTEAD WAS ABSORBED BY GALACTUS. OR PERHAPS...

...GALACTUS HAD BEEN ABSORBED BY IT.

MURDERER!

AAAAARRRRGGGHH!!!

I SAID...

...NOT IF I EAT YOU FIRST.

AND WITH THOSE WORDS IS BORN... EGO THE NECROWORLD.

THE BUTCHER OF GALACTUS.

HHRRGGH!!! NOOO!!! GAAAAARRGH!!!

AND SO THE STORY AT THE END OF TIME TAKES A TURN AND CONTINUES ON. AND WHERE NEXT IT MIGHT LEAD, NO ONE CAN SAY.

NO ONE AT ALL.

HEH.

I BELIEVE I SEE AN ENDING IN SIGHT FOR US, BROTHER.

AT LONG LAST.

LOKI HAS OFTEN TRIED TO WEAVE HIS OWN TALE, BUT THE PRINCE OF LIES IS ABOUT AS MUCH A NORN...AS HE IS A GIANT.

WELL, THAT WAS CONSIDERABLY LESS FUN THAN I THOUGHT IT WOULD BE.

I TOLD YOU WE WERE MEETING AN ENVOY OF MOUNTAIN GIANTS. WHAT EXACTLY WERE YOU EXPECTING TO HAPPEN, LITTLE PRINCE OF JACKASSES?

I SUPPOSE I THOUGHT THERE'D BE MORE FEASTING. THE ASGARDIANS DO LOVE THEIR FEASTS WHEN TREATING WITH ENVOYS.

ALSO I DIDN'T EXPECT YOUR GUARDS TO BE COMPLETELY WIPED OUT AND FOR US TO ALMOST BE MURDERED AND DEVOURED BY FLESH-EATING HILLBILLY GIANTS.

COWARDS AMBUSHED US. REAL GIANTS FIGHT FACE-TO-FACE. YOU'D KNOW THAT, BOY, IF YOU WERE MY SON IN MORE THAN NAME.

YES, WELL, AT LEAST THIS FINALLY AFFORDS US SOME TIME ALONE.

THERE ARE SO MANY QUESTIONS I'VE WANTED TO ASK YOU SINCE YOU CAME BACK TO LIFE, FATHER.

LIKE... OH, I DON'T KNOW...

IS IT TRUE MY MOTHER FARBAUTI BURIED AN ICE DAGGER IN HER OWN HEART THE NIGHT I WAS BORN?

OR... OR DID YOU...

UM, KING LAUFEY?

THIS DOESN'T STRIKE ME AS A PARTICULARLY GOOD PLACE FOR A NAP.

MIDGARD.
NEW YORK'S CENTRAL PARK.

While there are those like Loki who attempt to weave their own tale, there are others who are perfectly content letting the Norns weave it for them, as the gods intended.

This sometimes makes for unexpected plot twists.

The life of Simon Walterson is one such tale. Cursed by a mystic, he lost his human form.

And then a chance encounter with the God of Thunder transformed him even further.

THROG.
FROG OF THUNDER.

Hmm, no sign of the Upper West Side horde. Maybe the Rat Wars have finally ended.

Wait, what's that? Something lying in the grass. Looks almost like...

By the Spire of Belvedere Castle! This...

...this doesn't look like a job for the Frog of Thunder.

Does it?

"FOR ALL THE *THORS*."

RRGGGH! MJOLNIR! I'M DOWN HERE! I'M...

NO! I'M STARTING TO *CHANGE.* AS JANE, I'LL INSTANTLY BE CRUSHED TO DEATH.

MJOLNIR! HAVE TO TOUCH MJOLNIR OR I'LL...

MJOLNIR?

WOULD YOU SETTLE FOR A *SLIVER* OF IT?

MUST BE... PASSING OUT. BECAUSE I SWEAR THAT *FROG...*

...FROG LOOKS JUST LIKE...

"OH NO, NOT AGAIN."

I BLACKED OUT AGAIN. I...

YOU'RE LOSING IT, JENNIFER.

I'VE GOT TO GET SOME HELP BEFORE...BEFORE I HURT SOMEONE OTHER THAN MYSELF.

WOW. I CAN'T BELIEVE I JUST TEAMED UP WITH THE NEW THOR.

THIS... THIS CALLS FOR A CELEBRATION.

I WONDER WHERE I CAN FIND SOME MEAD?

REEEK

AH, SO YOU THINK ME AN EASY MEAL, DO YOU? YOU'LL SOON LEARN OTHERWISE.

RATS OF QUEENS, PREPARE TO TASTE THE HAMMER OF THROG!

REEEK

REEEK

REEEK

REEEK

HRRGH!
GET BACK,
YOU...!

NO, YOU
CANNOT HAVE
IT BACK! IT CHOSE
ME! IT CAME
TO ME! IT...

IT WANTS
ME TO END THE
WAR. AND I...I
WANT...

...YOU...
GOAT.

TOOTHGNASHER.

ODINSON
LEFT YOU TO
GUARD THE
HAMMER, DIDN'T
HE?

I NEVER
ASKED FOR
THIS! I NEVER
ASKED TO BE
THOR!

WOOM

WHAT IN THE NAME OF THE...GNASHER, NO, WAIT!

RRRRRAAAR!!

RRGH

BY ALL THE GODS. IT CAN'T BE.

YOU CALL YOURSELF THOR.

YOU'RE NO THOR I'VE EVER SEEN.

SKRRNNNCH

BUT YOU'LL DO.

THUNK

FOR A START.

THE WRATH OF THE MANGOG

THEY SAY IT IS FEROCITY PERSONIFIED.

RRRGGGH!!!

THEY SAY NOTHING THAT LIVES, NOTHING THAT BREATHES, CAN STAY ITS WRATH.

THAT IT HAS POWER FEW CAN COMPREHEND AND NONE CAN HOPE TO EQUAL.

THE POWER OF UNTOLD BILLIONS OF BEINGS.

THEY SAY IT WAS BORN FROM THE RAGE OF AN ENTIRE SLAUGHTERED PEOPLE.

AND ALL OF THOSE WONDERFUL THINGS ARE QUITE TRUE.

BUT THEY ARE NOT THE WHOLE OF THE TRUTH.

KRRRRNGG

GUUGH!

I DO NOT KNOW YOU. BUT YOU SMELL LIKE ONE OF THEM.

THE ASGARDIANS.

YOU ARE A GOD.

HRRGH.

THAT IS ALL I NEED TO KNOW.

THEY SAY THAT EONS AGO, A NOW LONG-FORGOTTEN RACE OF BEINGS **OFFENDED** THE VENERABLE **ALL-FATHER ODIN** FOR SOME REASON OR ANOTHER.

PERHAPS THEY RUTHLESSLY INVADED ASGARD.

KRRDKK

PERHAPS ONE OF THEM MERELY SPOKE THE WRONG WORD WHILE IN THE ALL-FATHER'S PRESENCE.

EITHER WAY, WE'LL NEVER KNOW FOR CERTAIN...

...SINCE ODIN'S RESPONSE WAS TO **SLAUGHTER** THEM ALL.

AN ENTIRE RACE WIPED OUT BY ONE IRATE DEITY.

BILLIONS OF BEINGS.

I AM NOT JUST... A GOD.

BUT SO GREAT WAS THEIR COLLECTIVE RAGE, THEIR UNBRIDLED HATRED, THAT IT DID NOT DISSIPATE WHEN THEY DIED.

I AM THE **WAR THOR.**

IT BECAME... SOMETHING ELSE.

THE GOD OF THE **BLOODSTORM!**

HAVE AT THEE, YOU BASTARD!

AND THUS MANGOG WAS BORN.

OR SO THE STORY GOES.

KRAKKADDOOOM

OVER THE YEARS, THE BEAST HAS COME TO ANNIHILATE ASGARD MANY TIMES, LAYING WASTE TO ENTIRE ARMIES OF GODS, STRIKING FEAR INTO EVEN THE COLD, OMNIPOTENT HEART OF ODIN HIMSELF.

BUT THE MANGOG'S RAMPAGE HAS ALWAYS ENDED IN UTTER DEFEAT.

ONCE ODIN EVEN RESURRECTED THE ENTIRE MURDERED RACE IN ORDER TO SATIATE MANGOG'S RAGE.

YET STILL THE GREAT MONSTER RETURNS, SOMEHOW ALWAYS STRONGER THAN HE WAS BEFORE.

BECAUSE MANGOG, IT SEEMS, HAS BECOME ABOUT MORE THAN JUST ONE WRONGED RACE.

HE IS JUDGMENT FOR THOSE WHO CANNOT BE JUDGED BY MAN.

THE MANGOG IS THE ULTIMATE JUDGMENT OF ALL THE GODS.

BUT NO GOD IN ALL THE REALMS FREELY CONSENTS TO JUDGMENT. NOT WITHOUT A FIGHT.

VANAHEIM.
REALM OF THE OLD GODS.

STRIKE TEAM DELTA TO ROXXON CONTROL, WE HAVE ENGAGED THE ENEMY. I REPEAT, WE HAVE ENGAGED THE ENEMY.

AND THE ENEMY IS KICKING OUR TAILS!

THESE DAMN *VANIR GODS* ARE OVERWHELMING US! WE COULD USE SOME REINFORCEMENTS DOWN HERE, A-S-A-DAMN-P!

COPY THAT, STRIKE TEAM. REINFORCEMENTS EN ROUTE.

B.E.R.S.E.R.K.E.R. SQUAD DEPLOYED.

ALL RIGHT, YOU MAGGOTS...!

GET READY TO SMASH SOME GODS!

CONTROL TO BLACK RAIN. WE'VE GOT GODS IN THE TREELINE, AND OUR BOYS ON THE GROUND ARE PRAYING FOR SOME HOLY BRIMSTONE.

COPY THAT.

PRAYERS ANSWERED. COURTESY OF 5,000 POUNDS OF NAPALM.

AND THE ROXXON ENERGY CORPORATION. HALLOWED BE THY NAME.

WHEN A **PRAYER** IS SENT OUT INTO THE ETHER... LIKE A DESPERATE CRY FOR HELP...AND IS PROMPTLY IGNORED BY ALL THE GODS...

...THE MANGOG KNOWS.

WHEN DEVOUT MEN DIE WHILE THEIR GODS DO NOTHING, THE MANGOG RISES.

WHEN DIVINE GARDENERS NEGLECT THEIR ORCHARDS AND ENTIRE WORLDS WITHER AND DIE, THE MANGOG RAGES.

UGGH.

WHEN THEY SIN AND CALL IT HOLY, HE SWELLS WITH POWER.

AND THEN HE COMES FOR THEM.

HGGGGHK!

WITH SOME SINS OF HIS OWN.

UGGH. IMPOSSIBLE.

I *EAT* THE IMPOSSIBLE.

AND THE OMNIPOTENT.

I FEED ON THE MONSTERS WHO HIDE IN HEAVEN. I AM THE GREAT MAGGOT GNAWING ITS WAY THROUGH THE ROTTING FLESH OF THE UNHOLIEST OF HOLIES.

FEEDING WITH THE HUNGER OF A BILLION BILLION BEINGS.

AND I HUNGER STILL.

NIFFLEHEIM.
LAND OF THE DEAD.

MMGH. I FEEL SO... STRANGE.

YOU'VE JUST ARRIVED. THE FEELING WILL PASS.

ARRIVED? LAST THING I REMEMBER...WAS THE *NORNKEEP* COLLAPSING AND THE *ODINSON...*

WHERE... WHERE *AM* I?

I AM TRULY AND DEEPLY SORRY, *QUEEN KARNILLA*, BUT...

WELCOME TO *HEL.*

HEL? THEN...

...I *DIED*. I DIED IN THAT RUBBLE.

I AM AFRAID YOU DID.

WAIT... *WHO*...WHO ARE...

BALDER? BALDER THE BRAVE...IS THAT REALLY YOU?

AYE, KARNILLA. THOUGH THESE DAYS IT'S *KING BALDER*, LORD OF CORPSES.

I IMAGINE YOU HAVE MANY QUESTIONS, MY LADY, BUT I'M AFRAID NOW IS NOT THE TIME FOR--

OH, MY LOVE. AT LONG LAST.

KARNILLA...

IT WAS WORTH IT. IT WAS WORTH *DYING* JUST TO SEE YOU AGAIN. I'VE MISSED YOU MORE THAN I COULD EVER--

RRRGGGH.

EASY, BOYS.

WHAT IN THE NAME OF THE NORNS ARE THOSE?

THE GUARDIANS OF NASTROND. WORRY NOT. THEY FIGHT FOR ME.

THEN WHY ARE THEY LOOKING AT ME LIKE THAT?

I IMAGINE THEY THOUGHT YOU WERE ATTACKING THEIR KING. THEY'RE NOT USED TO SEEING *HUGS* IN HEL.

COME, MY LADY--

RRRRROOOOOOORR!!!

WAR.

MUST STOP...THE WAR. CANNOT... FALL.

YOU ARE TOUGH. FOR GODMEAT. I WILL GIVE YOU THAT.

PERHAPS YOU REALLY DO FIGHT WITH THE POWER OF AN ENTIRE MURDERED UNIVERSE.

BUT MY RAGE COMES FROM INSIDE. WHILE YOURS...

...COMES FROM THIS.

n-no.

THE MANGOG WILL NEVER BREAK.

BUT THE SAME CANNOT BE SAID...FOR HAMMERS.

WHAT ARE YOU... GAAAARRGGH!!!

KRRRRRNNGGCH

AAAAARRRGGGHH!!

no.

no no no. HOW DID YOU...

NO MORE HAMMER.

NO MORE THOR.

WHERE?

BIG GOLDEN CITY, FLOATING NEAR SATURN. YOU CAN'T MISS IT.

AND *YOU* ARE...?

NOT A GOD. THUS NOT YOUR CONCERN.

THEN DON'T GET IN MY WAY.

OH, I WOULDN'T DREAM OF IT.

HELP.

PERHAPS SOMEDAY WE'LL LIVE IN A WORLD WHERE THE MANGOG IS NO LONGER NEEDED.

I'M CHANGING, I CAN'T... HOLD...

OH, WHY BOTHER HOLDING ON? THERE'S NOTHING HERE FOR YOU ANYMORE.

WHERE HIS RAGE CAN BE SATED FOREVER.

HELLO, WAR THOR.

I'M THAT *WAR* YOU'VE BEEN LOOKING FOR.

WHAT A BORING WORLD THAT WOULD BE.

I PREFER THE WORLD I'VE MADE, IN ALL ITS RUINED BEAUTY.

THE WORLD OF MALEKITH THE ACCURSED.

A WORLD ERUPTING WITH WAR.

A WORLD WHERE GODS ARE DYING.

WITH MORE SOON TO FOLLOW.

GODSPEED, MANGOG.

AND GOODBYE, MIGHTY THOR.

THE LAST DAYS OF THE GODDESS OF THUNDER

THE FORESTS OF VANAHEIM ARE OVERRUN WITH HULKED-OUT ROXXON SUPER-SOLDIERS. NUCLEAR BOMBS RAIN DOWN ON THE ANCIENT HOME OF THE GODS.

I SHOULD BE THERE.

IN JOTUNHEIM, THE GIANTS ARE AT WAR.

STORM AND MOUNTAIN GIANTS HAVE JOINED FORCES AGAINST THE FROST GIANTS. A LOSS FOR KING LAUFEY COULD TURN THE TIDE OF WAR.

I HAVE TO GET BACK THERE.

IN RUINED ALFHEIM, THE LIGHT ELVES ARE STARVING.

IF I DON'T HELP THEM, MORE AND MORE WILL DIE.

ULIK'S TROLLS ARE ATTACKING THE DWARF FORGES IN NIDAVELLIR.

THE ANGELS OF HEVEN HAVE WITHDRAWN FROM THE CONGRESS OF WORLDS. THE QUEEN OF THE NORNS IS DEAD.

THERE ARE SO MANY REALMS IN PERIL. AND SO FEW THUNDER GODS.

THE DUSK LANDS OF NIFFLEHEIM ARE BEING INVADED BY QUEEN SINDR AND HER FIRE GOBLIN ARMY.

I HAVE VOWED TO THE KING OF HEL TO FIGHT ALONGSIDE THE DEAD.

I CAN'T REMEMBER THE LAST TIME I DID SOMETHING EVEN REMOTELY RESEMBLING SLEEP. OR WHEN I LAST PUT DOWN THIS HAMMER.

BUT THERE ISN'T TIME TO BE ANYTHING OTHER THAN THOR. NOT AS LONG AS THE WAR OF THE REALMS IS STILL RAGING.

AND NOW, TO TRY AND WIN THAT PEACE, THERE'S ONE VERY IMPORTANT THING I MUST DO NEXT.

HE CAN GO ON AND ON FOR CENTURIES ABOUT THOSE. AND WE DO NOT HAVE THAT KIND OF TIME.

YOU! I KNEW YOU WERE *UNWORTHY*, BUT THIS IS A NEW LOW. IS THERE NO HONOR AMONG THORS THESE DAYS?

ODINSON, WHY DID YOU DO THAT? I HAD HIM BEAT.

THERE IS NO POINT MEASURING EGOS AGAINST HERCULES. BELIEVE ME, I KNOW.

THIS ISN'T ABOUT EGO.

IT'S ABOUT ENDING THE WAR. IT'S ABOUT THE GODS OF OLYMPUS DOING THE RIGHT THING.

HA, DON'T LISTEN TO HIM, MY LADY. HE'S ONLY SORE BECAUSE YOU GAVE ME MORE OF A *CHALLENGE* THAN HE EVER DID.

AND WORRY NOT...

EVEN THOUGH I WAS ON THE IMMINENT VERGE OF SOUNDLY DEFEATING YOU...

I WILL STILL GRANT YOUR BOON.

I WILL TELL MY FATHER WHAT YOU'VE TOLD ME ABOUT THIS...WAR OF THE REALMS AND ASK FOR THE GODS OF OLYMPUS TO INTERVENE.

I WARN YOU, THOUGH, IT WILL NOT BE AN EASY TASK. SKYFATHER ZEUS IS JUST AS STUBBORN AS THE ONE-EYED ALL-FATHER OF ASGARD.

BUT I PROMISE YOU, MY LADY, THAT NO MATTER THE JUDGMENT OF ZEUS AND NO MATTER WHAT MANNER OF FEARSOME FOES YOU MAY FIND ARRAYED BEFORE YOU...

AT LEAST *ONE* GOD OF OLYMPUS WILL BE THERE TO FIGHT BY YOUR SIDE.

AND HIS NAME IS HERCULES, PRINCE OF POWER.

WHAT IN THE REALMS HAS THAT SORT OF POWER?

THE SAME THING THAT HAD THE POWER TO REND HIS HAMMER TO PIECES.

AND TO... TO TEAR *TOOTHGNASHER'S* HEAD FROM HIS BODY.

I'VE HEARD WHISPERS. I KNOW IT'S SOMETHING THAT EVEN THE GODS FEAR.

AYE. WITH GOOD REASON.

ON PREVIOUS OCCASIONS, IT HAS DEFEATED THE ARMIES OF ASGARD ALL BY ITSELF AND ALMOST BROUGHT ABOUT *RAGNAROK* THROUGH THE SHEER FORCE OF ITS OWN MONSTROUS WILL.

AND NOW, I BELIEVE THE MANGOG HAS RETURNED, TO JUDGE THE GODS ANEW.

OH, ODINSON. I AM SO SORRY.

VOLSTAGG HAS NOT SPOKEN A WORD. AND MAY NEVER DO SO AGAIN.

BUT THE ROYAL VIZIERS HAVE RECENTLY FORESEEN THIS MOMENT. AND *KARNILLA* SPOKE OF IT WITH HER DYING WORDS.

TELL ME, THOR...HAVE YOU EVER HEARD TELL OF THE *MANGOG?*

EVEN THE ALL-SEEING *HEIMDALL* CANNOT FIND IT, BUT I KNOW THE MANGOG IS COMING TO ASGARDIA--COMING FOR ALL OF US. THE GODS MUST BE READY.

WHEN IT COMES, WE WILL FACE IT TOGETHER. BUT UNTIL THEN... THERE IS A *WAR* RAGING ACROSS THE REALMS--

NOT FOR *YOU*, THERE ISN'T.

THE ONLY WAR YOU SHOULD BE FACING IS THE ONE RAGING INSIDE YOU.

UNHAND ME, ODINSON, OR LOSE THE ONLY HAND YOU HAVE LEFT.

IF I MUST *FIGHT* TO KEEP YOU HERE, I WILL.

THEN YOU WOULD BE FIGHTING ON THE SIDE OF *MALEKITH.*

NO--OF *LIFE.* FOR MY MORTAL FRIEND, *JANE FOSTER.*

DO YOU STILL REMEMBER *HER,* GODDESS OF THUNDER?

LAST TIME I SAW HER, SHE WAS IN DESPERATE NEED OF MEDICAL CARE.

AYE. WHEN SHE SHOULD HAVE BEEN UNDERGOING TREATMENT FOR HER CANCER.

SHE IS FINE. SHE ARM-WRESTLED A GOD TODAY.

THERE... THERE ISN'T TIME TO BE SICK.

THAT IS THE HAMMER TALKING. NOT THE DOCTOR WHO WIELDS IT.

THIS IS WHY THE HAMMER CHOSE ME.

THAT DOESN'T MEAN YOU HAVE TO LET IT KILL YOU.

IF THAT IS WHAT IT TAKES TO SAVE THE REALMS, I AM NOT AFRAID TO DIE.

THEN DON'T BE AFRAID TO *LIVE.*

IT'S NOT SEDITION, CUL. IT'S COMMON SENSE. TOO BAD YOU'RE NOT THE GOD OF *THAT*.

AND YOU'RE NOT A *SENATOR* ANYMORE, JANE FOSTER. YOU'RE JUST SOME HALF-DEAD MORTAL WHO DOESN'T BELONG HERE.

LEAVE NOW, OR YOU WILL BE TREATED AS AN ENEMY OF ASGARD.

IF THAT'S YOUR PLAN, SERPENT, YOU'RE GOING TO NEED MORE GUARDS. AND ANOTHER *HEAD*, BY THE TIME I'M DONE WITH YOU.

IT DOESN'T MATTER WHAT YOU DO TO ME, CUL. THE WAR IS STILL COMING. THE PILLARS OF THE REALM ETERNAL WILL SHAKE, ONE WAY OR THE OTHER.

SO WHY WAIT? I SAY IT'S TIME WE GAVE THEM A GOOD SHAKING OURSELVES!

AYE! DOWN WITH CUL! DOWN WITH THE BORSON BROTHERS!

EVERY GOD DESERVES A VOICE! WE DEMAND TO BE HEARD!

REVOLUTION! DEATH TO THE PATRIARCHY! SMITING AND MORE SMITING!

KROOMM

SQUAWK

SQUAWK

ENOUGH!!!

AND SO IT BEGINS.

OVER THE EONS, THESE ALL-SEEING EYES HAVE WATCHED WORLDS CRUMBLE AND GALAXIES BURN.

THEY'VE BEHELD SLAUGHTER, INJUSTICE AND TRAGEDY ON THE GRANDEST, MOST COSMIC OF SCALES.

THEY'VE SEEN WAR AFTER WAR AFTER WAR. BUT WHAT COMES NEXT...

...WILL BE DIFFICULT TO WATCH.

THE FALL OF ASGARD

WHAT HAPPENED?

YOU *COLLAPSED.* I RUSHED YOU HERE TO MIDGARD AND ALERTED *SENATOR SOLOMON.*

AND *I* CALLED IN THE CAVALRY. YOU NEVER SHOULDA TOLD ME WHO ALL KNEW YOUR BIG SECRET, DOC.

FALCON? DR. STRANGE? I...

DON'T TALK, JANE. JUST LISTEN. PLEASE.

CONSIDER THIS AN INTERVENTION, DR. FOSTER. ON BEHALF OF PEOPLE WHO LOVE AND RESPECT YOU. AND WHO REFUSE TO WATCH YOU MURDER YOURSELF. ONE PEAL OF THUNDER AT A TIME.

I KNOW HOW DIFFICULT IT IS TO LET GO OF BEING THOR. IN THE NAME OF ALL THE GODS, DO I KNOW!

BUT THAT IS WHAT *MUST* HAPPEN HERE TODAY, LADY JANE. AT LEAST UNTIL YOU HAVE MADE YOURSELF HEALTHY ONCE MORE.

BUT... ASGARDIA--

--IS NOT YOUR CONCERN. KICKING CANCER'S ASS IS ALL YOU NEED TO BE WORRIED ABOUT. BELIEVE ME, JANE...

WHEN THE GODS ARE KNOWN FOR HONOR AND COMPASSION OVER ARROGANCE AND CRUELTY, *THEN* WILL MANGOG STOP!

IN OTHER WORDS, *NEVER*!

HOFUND! MY SWORD!

YOU ARE THE ONLY CRUEL ONE HERE, YOU--

YOU SEE VERY LITTLE FOR AN ALL-SEEING GOD, DON'T YOU? TELL ME, MIGHTY HEIMDALL...

HRRGGH!

DID YOU FORESEE *THIS*?!

AAAAAHHHH!

I...I AM THE GOD OF FEAR. BUT NEVER HAVE I SEEN IT IN MY OWN BROTHER'S EYES. UNTIL *TODAY*.

YMIR'S BLOODY BONES.

LORD CUL... THE BEAST CANNOT BE STOPPED.

IF EVEN THE *ALL-FATHER* FEARS THIS MANGOG, THEN...

THE BIFROST! TRIGGER THE BIFROST!

SEND THE BEAST OUT OF HERE!

THANK YOU FOR ALLOWING ME TO EXAMINE YOU LIKE THIS, DOCTOR.

LIKE I SAID, JUST DON'T GO TRYING ANY MAGICAL CURES.

I UNDERSTAND.

ARE YOU SURE YOU WOULDN'T LIKE THE REST OF US TO LEAVE THE ROOM?

NO, LET'S JUST GET THIS OVER WITH. TELL ME WHAT I ALREADY KNOW, DR. STRANGE.

WELL, I WAS NO ONCOLOGIST IN MY PREVIOUS DAY JOB, BUT I KNOW BETTER THAN ANYONE THE EFFECT *MYSTICAL FORCES* CAN HAVE ON THE BODY.

WHEN THIS ALL BEGAN, OVER A YEAR AGO, YOUR INITIAL CANCER TREATMENTS WERE SHOWING *POSITIVE* RESULTS, WEREN'T THEY, DR. FOSTER?

IT WAS STAGE ONE BREAST CANCER. YOUR PHYSICIANS FELT CONFIDENT YOUR LUMPECTOMY HAD REMOVED ALL THE CANCEROUS CELLS AND THAT YOUR CHEMOTHERAPY WOULD KEEP IT FROM SPREADING.

BUT THEN SOMETHING SUDDENLY *CHANGED.* SOMETHING THE DOCTORS COULD NEVER EXPLAIN.

SUDDENLY YOUR TREATMENTS WERE INEFFECTIVE. YOUR CANCER METASTASIZED, SPREADING TO YOUR LYMPH NODES. STAGE ONE BECAME STAGE TWO.

ANOTHER ROUND OF CHEMOTHERAPY WAS EVEN LESS EFFECTIVE, ESPECIALLY SINCE YOU DIDN'T ALWAYS SHOW UP FOR TREATMENT.

IT'S IN YOUR LIVER NOW AS WELL. STAGE FOUR. ADVANCED METASTIC CANCER.

WHAT CHANGED WAS THAT YOU FOUND A *MAGIC HAMMER* ON THE MOON. YOU BECAME THE MIGHTY *THOR,* GODDESS OF THUNDER.

AND THE MORE YOU SAVED THE WORLD, THE MORE YOU WERE *KILLING* YOURSELF.

... JUST PROMISE ME ONE THING...

ANYTHING IN ALL THE HEAVENS.

YOU'RE ALL *SOLDIERS* NOW. I'M OFFICIALLY SWEARING YOU IN.

SOLDIERS IN THE *WAR OF THE REALMS.*

MAKE SURE OUR SIDE DOESN'T LOSE.

GO! GET OUT OF HERE, MJOLNIR!

AND DON'T COME BACK UNTIL RAGNAROK!

"THIS MOMENT... WAS INEVITABLE.

"I'VE KNOWN THAT FOR A VERY LONG TIME.

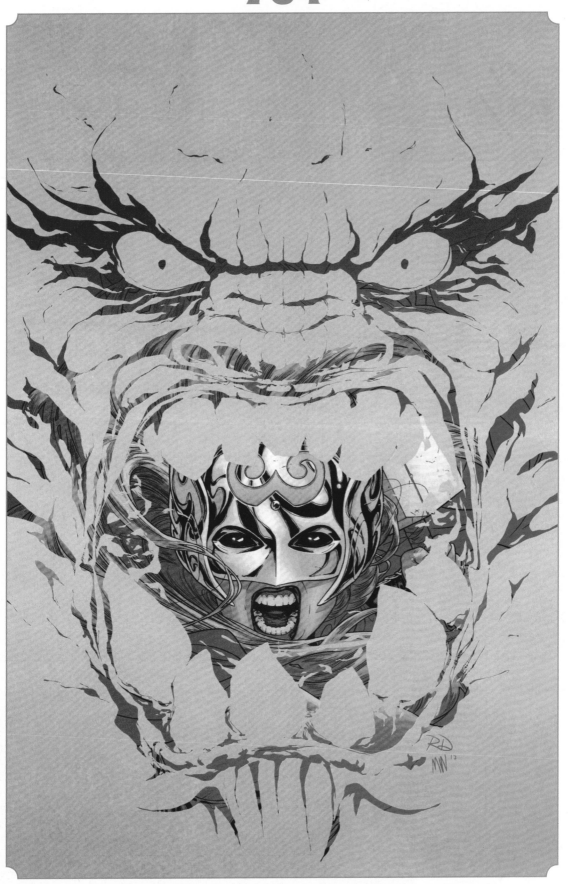

THE GOSPEL ACCORDING TO JANE

I NEVER STARTED GOING TO CHURCH LIKE MY MOTHER WANTED.

AT FIRST, I WAS JUST TOO ANGRY ABOUT LOSING HER. MY DAD AND I BOTH WERE.

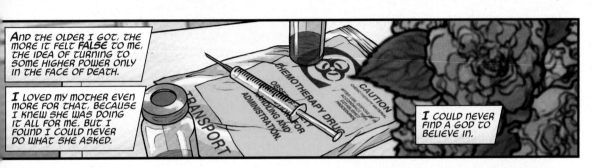

AND THE OLDER I GOT, THE MORE IT FELT FALSE TO ME, THE IDEA OF TURNING TO SOME HIGHER POWER ONLY IN THE FACE OF DEATH.

I LOVED MY MOTHER EVEN MORE FOR THAT, BECAUSE I KNEW SHE WAS DOING IT ALL FOR ME. BUT I FOUND I COULD NEVER DO WHAT SHE ASKED.

I COULD NEVER FIND A GOD TO BELIEVE IN.

INSTEAD THE GODS FOUND ME.

BUT THERE ARE NO GODS HERE NOW FOR ME TO LEAN ON. OR SIPHON AWAY THEIR POWER TO MAKE ME STRONGER.

AND I'VE GOT NO FAMILY LEFT, NO ONE I'M LEAVING BEHIND. THERE'S JUST ME.

AND THAT'LL HAVE TO BE ENOUGH.

MY NAME IS JANE FOSTER.

AND IF THIS IS THE STORY OF HOW I DIE... THEN KNOW THAT IT WON'T END...

LOKI...

I'M HERE TO *HELP* WITH THAT. I'M THE *SORCERER SUPREME* OF MIDGARD NOW, MOTHER.

I CAN SEND YOU FAR ENOUGH AWAY THAT THE MANGOG WILL HAVE TO SEARCH FOR A MILLION YEARS TO--

HOW *DARE* YOU SHOW YOUR FACE HERE! ESPECIALLY TO *ME*!

HAVE YOU COME TO BURY ANOTHER POISONED DAGGER IN MY BACK? SINCE THE FIRST ONE FAILED TO DO THE JOB?

MOTHER...

STOP CALLING ME THAT! YOU'VE LOST ALL RIGHTS TO USE THAT WORD!

LADY FREYJA.

IF I'D WANTED THAT DAGGER TO KILL YOU...DO YOU REALLY THINK YOU'D BE STANDING HERE INSTEAD OF IN VALHALLA?

MALEKITH WANTED ASGARD IN THE HANDS OF *ODIN*, NOT YOU. BECAUSE HE KNEW THE ALL-FATHER WOULD KEEP IT ISOLATED AND OUT OF HIS WAR OF THE REALMS.

MALEKITH AND HIS CABAL WERE DETERMINED TO SEE YOU *DEAD*. I KNEW YOU'D NEVER WILLINGLY STEP ASIDE. NOT EVEN TO SAVE YOUR OWN LIFE.

SO...I MADE THE HARD CHOICE FOR YOU.

I HAVE BEEN IN A *COMA* FOR MONTHS. ON THE VERY *EDGE* OF DEATH. WHILE *WAR* WAS RAMPAGING THROUGH THE REALMS, KILLING *THOUSANDS.*

DO YOU EXPECT ME TO *THANK* YOU FOR THAT?

NO, I NEVER EXPECTED THAT.

EVERYONE TOLD ME I WAS A FOOL FOR YET AGAIN DARING TO TRUST YOU. FOR GIVING YOU ONE LAST CHANCE TO PROVE YOURSELF.

TO SHOW THAT THE GOOD I SAW INSIDE YOU WASN'T A RUSE. THAT YOUR HONOR COULD FINALLY OUTWEIGH YOUR GODFORSAKEN LIES.

BUT THEY WERE *RIGHT,* WEREN'T THEY? WITH YOU, LOKI... THE LIES ALWAYS WIN IN THE END.

IT'S NO LIE WHEN I TELL YOU THAT ASGARDIA WILL FALL TODAY.

AND NO ONE, NO GOD IN ALL THE HEAVENS, CAN DO ANYTHING TO CHANGE THAT.

NOT THE ALL-FATHER.

NOT THE ODINSON.

NOT *YOU.*

THERE ARE SOME THINGS... YOU JUST CAN'T SAVE.

GOODBYE, LADY FREYJA.

KEITH, MY EX-HUSBAND. JIMMY, MY...MY SON. BOTH ARE...

KEITH MUST'VE FALLEN ASLEEP AT THE WHEEL. CAR WENT THROUGH THE GUARDRAIL.

WHERE WERE YOU, THOR?

WHERE WAS ODIN OR SIF OR HERCULES? THERE ARE MORE OF YOU OUT THERE THAN I CAN COUNT. ALWAYS MEDDLING IN OUR LIVES WHEN IT SUITS YOU.

WHERE WERE ANY OF YOU TONIGHT?

WHERE... WHERE WAS I?

"FIND A GOD TO BELIEVE IN." I TRIED, MOTHER. I DID.

JANE...

BUT I DON'T THINK THEY BELIEVE IN US.

AND I DON'T BLAME THEM.

HEY, BONNIE.

DR. FOSTER. HAVEN'T SEEN YOU IN A WHILE.

IN THIS WARD, I GET WORRIED WHEN I DON'T SEE FOLKS FOR A WHILE.

I'M STILL KICKING. HOW ABOUT YOU?

EH, THE NURSES TELL ME I'M STILL ALIVE. BUT SOME DAYS I AIN'T SO SURE.

I TOLD YOU, BONNIE, YOU GOTTA BE AROUND TO KEEP THAT *FLOWER* ALIVE, AFTER ALL THE TROUBLE I WENT THROUGH.

CARPATHIAN *SNOW ROSE*. THE RAREST FLOWER IN THE WORLD. ONLY GROWS ATOP THE HIGHEST MOUNTAIN IN LATVERIA. I STILL DON'T KNOW HOW YOU GOT IT.

OH, YOU KNOW...THE INTERNET.

I'M JUST GLAD TO SEE YOU AND IT ARE BOTH LOOKING BEAUTIFUL.

I DON'T WANNA KEEP YOU, BONNIE. I JUST WANTED TO STOP IN.

WOULD YOU *PRAY* WITH ME, DOCTOR, BEFORE YOU GO?

...

DOC?

YEAH.

OF COURSE I WOULD.

JUST TELL ME WHO WE'RE PRAYING TO, BONNIE.

LOOK, I'M TELLING YOU, THERE'S SOMETHING GOING ON UP THERE.

YEAH, I KNOW MY SECURITY CLEARANCE EXPIRED WHEN S.H.I.E.L.D. WENT UNDER. CONSIDER THIS AN ANONYMOUS TIP IF YOU WANT, I DON'T CARE.

YOU'RE *ALPHA FLIGHT.* IT'S YOUR JOB TO PROTECT THE PLANET, RIGHT? SO JUST POINT SOME OF THOSE SATELLITES OF YOURS AT *ASGARDIA,* OKAY?

BECAUSE SOMETHING'S *WRONG.*

Level 8
Maria Wheelock Cancer Center

Infusion Room ↓
Family Lounge ↓
Patient Rooms ↓
K71 - K73 →
K74 - K86 ←

THE ODINSON LEFT LIKE A GOAT OUT OF HELL, AND NOW I CAN'T CALL THE BIFROST. WHICH MEANS *HEIMDALL'S* NOT WATCHING. AND HEIMDALL'S *ALWAYS* WATCHING. SO...

YEAH, IT'S OUT NEAR SATURN. A BIG GOLDEN CITY FLOATING IN SPACE. YOU CAN'T MISS--

WHAT DO YOU MEAN IT'S NOT THERE? OF COURSE IT'S THERE. IT'S...

PASSING *MARS?* WHY WOULD IT BE...

WAIT, YOU SAID IT'S ON A COURSE FOR *WHAT?*

PATCH ME THROUGH TO THE AVENGERS! ANY OF THEM!

DO IT NOW!

RAWF HAMMER!

RAWF RAWF MURDER!

I WOULD'VE *BEATEN* YOU, YOU LITTLE CANCEROUS SONS OF BITCHES.

SUNDOWN

TROUBLE **SLEEPING**, MY LADY?

MY WHOLE LIFE.

SLEEPING'S ALWAYS FELT TOO MUCH LIKE **DYING** TO ME. AND AS FAR AS I'M CONCERNED, I'VE HAD MY FILL OF BOTH.

YOU SOUND MORE LIKE AN ASGARDIAN EVERY DAY, SENATOR. YET EVEN THE GODS CANNOT AVOID SLUMBER, EITHER THE TEMPORARY OR THE PERMANENT VARIETY.

I DON'T SEE YOU SLEEPING, **HEIMDALL**.

AND I WOULD RATHER NOT SEE YOU **PERISH**, LADY JANE.

IN YOUR **CONDITION**--

MY CONDITION...IS A **RESTLESS** ONE. AND I IMAGINE WE BOTH KNOW WHY.

I HAVE A **VOICE** IN MY HEAD, HEIMDALL. AND I WON'T INSULT YOU BY LYING ABOUT WHAT IT WANTS ME TO DO.

JUST SEND ME THERE. BEFORE I COME TO MY SENSES.

YOU ARE A SENATOR IN THE **CONGRESS OF WORLDS**, JANE FOSTER. THE **BIFROST** IS YOURS TO COMMAND.

MAY THE GODS BE WITH YOU.

THOUGH PERHAPS YOU WOULD'VE BEEN FAR BETTER OFF...

"...IF THEY NEVER HAD BEEN."

THERE MUST ALWAYS BE A THOR.

...ever holds this hammer, if she be worthy, shall possess the power of... THOR

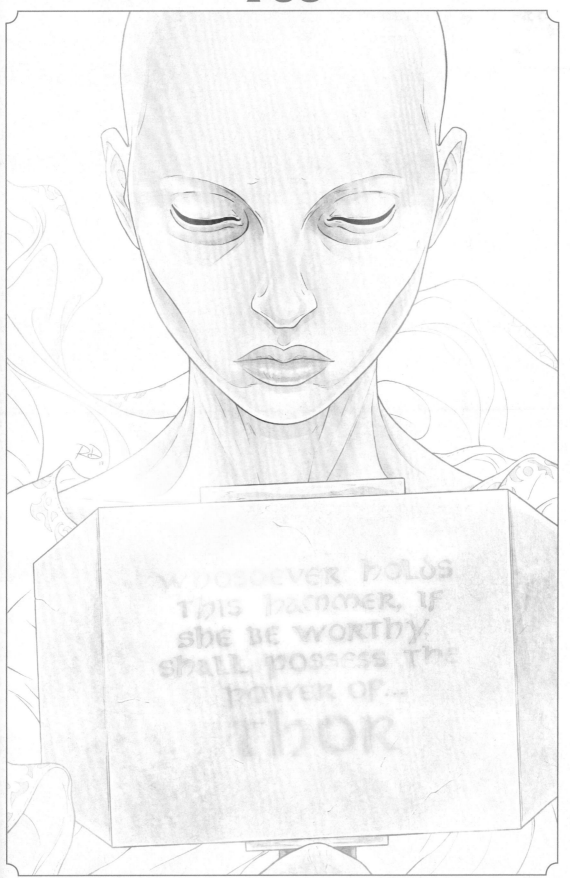

WHOSOEVER HOLDS this hammer, if she be worthy, shall possess the power of... Thor

AT THE GATES OF VALHALLA

"MAY SHE FIND HER WAY WITHOUT HASTE TO THE HALL OF THE HONORED SLAIN.

"MAY THE WARRIORS OF LEGEND WELCOME HER AS ONE OF THEIR OWN.

HELLO?

"MAY THE MEAD FLOW LIKE RIVERS THIS DAY AND ALL THE REST OF THE DAYS.

I...DON'T KNOW WHERE I AM. ASGARDIA WAS BURNING, AND... I WAS CHANGING, AND THEN... THEN I...

OH.

"MAY JANE FOSTER FEAST FOREVER IN *VALHALLA.*"

THE GATES OF VALHALLA. THAT...

THAT MEANS I'M...

YOU!

IT WAS YOU ALL ALONG!

ODIN...?

YOU STOLE THE HAMMER!

YOU ROBBED MY SON OF HIS BIRTHRIGHT! HIS VERY NAME!

YOU'VE BEEN THE SOURCE OF ALL MY TROUBLES FOR MONTHS NOW!!!

THAT'S NOT EXACTLY HOW IT--

YOU TURNED ALL OF ASGARD AGAINST ME!

ACTUALLY, YOU DID THAT ALL BY YOUR--

YOU EVEN DARED LAY YOUR HANDS AND HAMMER UPON ME, THE HOLY ALL-FATHER, IN PERSONAL COMBAT!

NOW THAT...I DID DO.

AND I'D DO IT ALL AG--

YOU...!

IT'S... BEAUTIFUL.

WHY DO YOU HESITATE? A GREAT FEAST IS ABOUT TO BEGIN, IN YOUR HONOR.

BE NOT AFRAID. YOU HAVE NOTHING MORE TO FEAR FROM ME OR ANYONE ELSE EVER AGAIN.

ALL WHO FALL VALIANTLY IN BATTLE ARE CHILDREN OF ODIN. SO TELL ME...

WHAT TROUBLES THEE, DAUGHTER JANE?

I... I WASN'T READY.

I WASN'T READY TO DIE.

WELL... WHAT DO YOU THINK?

I THINK IT'S A BROKEN, RUINED OLD MESS THAT HAS CLEARLY SEEN BETTER DAYS. IN OTHER WORDS...

IT'S A PRETTY PERFECT HOME FOR *ALL* OF US THESE DAYS.

OH, NAY. NOT FOR YOU.

THIS IS THE LAND WHERE I WAS BORN. HERE, IN TIME, THE GODS WILL REBUILD.

BUT *YOU* ARE GOING BACK TO *MIDGARD* ON THE NEXT AVAILABLE BOAT, JANE FOSTER. BACK TO THE *HOSPITAL* WHERE YOU BELONG.

RELAX, IT'S JUST A VISIT. BELIEVE IT OR NOT, I'M FINALLY BEING A GOOD PATIENT.

AS YOU SAID, NONE OF US ARE WHAT WE ONCE WERE, MY LADY.

WITH MJOLNIR NO MORE, I WILL EVER BE THE *UNWORTHY* PRINCE OF ASGARD. I WILL MAKE MY PEACE WITH THAT.

THE AGE OF THOR HAS *ENDED.*

THE AGE OF THOR WILL OUTLAST THE STARS.

WHEN THE *BIFROST* WAS DESTROYED, WE WERE CUT OFF FROM THE REST OF THE REALMS. BUT *MALEKITH* WASN'T.

THOSE REALMS ARE STILL AT WAR. AND THEIR MIGHTIEST PROTECTOR CANNOT ABANDON THEM.

HERE, TAKE THIS.

UUGH. ZOUNDS.

SO SMALL, BUT SO IMPOSSIBLY *HEAVY.* WHAT...

... IS THIS...

YES.

IT'S A PIECE OF MJOLNIR, FALLEN FROM THE SUN. I FOUND IT ON THE MOON, AFTER YOU BROUGHT ME BACK. AS FAR AS I KNOW, IT'S ALL THAT REMAINS OF THE HAMMER.

SUCH A SMALL PIECE. AND I CAN...*BARELY* HOLD IT.

THAT TELLS ME I COULD *NEVER* LIFT THE ENTIRE HAMMER. THAT I'M STILL NOT...

THE HAMMER MADE ME THE THUNDERER. BUT NOT YOU. *YOU* DID THAT YOURSELF.

ODINSON, LOOK AT ME...

"THERE MUST ALWAYS BE A THOR."

THAT'S WHAT I SAID RIGHT BEFORE I LIFTED MJOLNIR AND WAS TRANSFORMED FOR THE VERY FIRST TIME.

I WAS HONORED TO CARRY THAT MANTLE FOR A WHILE. HONORED THAT YOU BESTOWED UPON ME YOUR OWN NAME.

BUT IT'S TIME YOU *RECLAIMED* WHO YOU ARE.

THERE MUST ALWAYS BE A THOR.

AND NOW... ONCE AGAIN... IT MUST BE *YOU*.

BUT... I...

I SHOWED YOU WHAT I COULD BE WITH THAT HAMMER IN MY HAND.

NOW SHOW ME WHAT YOU CAN BE *WITHOUT* IT. SHOW US ALL.

I DO HAVE...A FEW IDEAS.

GODS, WOULD IT BE GREAT TO *FLY* AGAIN.

I LOVE YOU, JANE FOSTER.

YOU ARE MORE A GOD THAN I COULD EVER BE.

AND YOU'VE GOT MORE HUMANITY THAN MOST HUMANS I KNOW.

I LOVE YOU, TOO.

THOR.

HOGUN! WHERE ARE THOSE DWARVES?! AND ARE ANY OF THEM BLACKSMITHS?!

WE MURDER DWARVES?

NO, THORI, WE'VE HAMMERS TO BUILD!

VERY MANY HAMMERS!

THORS AND THEIR HAMMERS.

I GET IT NOW.

I'LL MISS THE FLYING, TOO.

THE END.

THE TOMORROW GIRLS
&
THE LORD OF THE REALMS

"THIS...ISN'T QUITE WHAT I EXPECTED.

"I THOUGHT THE BUILDINGS WOULD AT LEAST BE SOMEWHAT... *SHINIER.*"

AND THE PEOPLE WOULD BE A TAD LESS *DEAD.*

THIS IS WRONG. THIS DOESN'T LOOK AT ALL LIKE THE CORRECT TIME PERIOD. I THINK WE MISSED OUR MARK BY A FEW CENTURIES. WE'LL HAVE TO TRY AGAIN, AND THIS TIME--

HOLD, SISTER. LET US NOT BE HASTY. CORRECT TIME PERIOD OR NOT...

...I CAN SUDDENLY THINK OF ONE OR TWO REASONS TO STICK AROUND.

WHAT IS THIS? ARE THESE *VIKINGS* SO BEREFT OF WARRIORS THAT THEY'RE SENDING ARMED *CHILDREN* AGAINST US?

HA! THIS VILLAGE IS *OURS* NOW! BE GOOD LITTLE MAIDENS AND FETCH YOUR NEW MASTERS MORE MEAD!

ARE THOSE... *TROLLS?* LIKE... *PROPER* TROLLS?

THEY'RE EVEN UGLIER THAN GRANDFATHER DESCRIBED THEM.

YOU THERE! ARE YOU LOT TROLLS, OR SOME OTHER SORT OF ASTEROID-FACED, PREHISTORIC NIMRODS?

YES, WE'RE TROLLS, YOU IDIOT WHELPS! AND WHO IN THE NAME OF GRIMLOCK ARE *YOU?!*

ARE YOU SURE WE DIDN'T PUT TOO MUCH IN HIS MEAD?

HE LOOKS *DEAD.*

DEAD MEN DON'T TYPICALLY *SNORE* THAT LOUD.

WE USED THE EXACT RIGHT AMOUNT OF SLEEPING BERRIES. I MADE SURE OF IT. HE'LL BE OUT FOR HOURS. BUT WE SHOULDN'T WASTE TIME, SISTERS. LET'S GO.

"WASTE TIME." IS THAT YOUR IDEA OF A JEST, *ELLISIV?* IF THIS WORKS, WE'LL BE ABLE TO WASTE ALL THE TIME WE WANT. AND I CAN SKIP OVER EVERY BATH NIGHT FOR THE REST OF MY LIFE.

THIS IS NOTHING TO BE UNDERTAKEN LIGHTLY, *ATLI.* IF WE'RE NOT CAREFUL, WE COULD UNRAVEL THE VERY FABRIC OF THE UNIVERSE.

IF WE CAN UNDERTAKE IT AT ALL. YOU TRULY BELIEVE YOU'VE FINALLY FOUND A WAY?

LET ME GUESS. YOU FOUND IT IN A BORING OLD *BOOK.*

ASGARD IS MORE ANCIENT THAN ANY OF US CAN IMAGINE. FAR OLDER THAN EVEN *GRANDFATHER THOR.* ITS SECRETS ARE WITHOUT NUMBER.

WHILE YOU TWO SPEND YOUR TIME WHACKING METEORS AND CHASING STABLE BOYS, I'VE BEEN PAINSTAKINGLY *CATALOGUING* THOSE SECRETS.

AND TWO DAYS AGO, I FOUND *EXACTLY* WHAT WE'VE BEEN SEARCHING FOR.

I DOUBT EVEN THE ALL-GRANDFATHER REMEMBERS THIS ROOM EXISTS.

WHATEVER YOU DO, DON'T TOUCH ANYTHING UNLESS I SAY SO.

DIAMONDS? WHY WOULD WE NEED SHINY STONES? I CAN MAKE THOSE THINGS MYSELF WITH JUST MY HANDS AND A LUMP OF OLD SMOKE ROCK.

THESE ARE NO NORMAL GEMSTONES, *FRIGG.*

THESE ARE *TIME DIAMONDS.* GEMS THAT BEND THE VERY FABRIC OF TIME AND SPACE. ONE OF THE LOST WONDERS OF THE ANCIENT WORLD.

THE ANCIENT WORLD SURE WAS *WEIRD.*

SO WHAT DO WE DO? EAT THEM?

WELL...THE SCROLLS I FOUND IN THE ASGARDIAN LIBRARY...DIDN'T MENTION HOW EXACTLY TO *ACTIVATE* THEM.

BUT IF I WERE TO GUESS... I'D SAY WE JUST TAKE HOLD OF ONE, VERY CAREFULLY, AND ALL TOGETHER THINK OF WHERE WE--

TAKE US TO THE *GOLDEN AGE OF THOR!*

ATLI, NO! THAT'S NOT--

TROLLS! HOW DID I EVER LIVE THIS LONG WITHOUT TROLLS IN MY LIFE?!

TELL ME I CAN BRING SOME HOME WITH US!

ABSOLUTELY NOT! GODS, I HOPE WE'RE NOT CORRUPTING THE TIMESTREAM JUST BY SMITING THESE THINGS.

WHEN WE GET BACK TO OUR OWN TIME, WE'RE LIABLE TO FIND A TROLL SITTING ON THE THRONE OF ASGARD!

WHEN WE GET BACK TO OUR OWN TIME, ALL WE'LL FIND IS GRANDFATHER SNORING AWAY.

RELAX, ELLI. IN THIS DAY AND AGE, TROLLS GET SMITED EVERY DAY. JUST NOT USUALLY BY THE GODDESSES OF THUNDER.

ENJOY IT WHILE IT LASTS, SISTERS.

GAAGGGGH! THAT DIDN'T LAST LONG ENOUGH!

I WANT MORE TROLLS!

WE DON'T HAVE TIME TO SEARCH FOR MORE TROLLS. THE VILLAGE IS SAVED, WE DID OUR PART. NOW WE NEED TO BE LEAVING.

IS IT SAVED? IT STILL LOOKS LIKE A DUNG HEAP.

THIS IS THE VIKING AGE. THAT'S HOW IT'S SUPPOSED TO LOOK.

IF THIS IS THE VIKING AGE, THEN WHERE'S YOUNG THOR? THE ONE WITH THE AX WHO WE MET DURING THAT BUSINESS WITH THE GOD BUTCHER?*

YOU MEAN THE ONE ELLISIV THOUGHT WAS CUTE?

GODS, FOR THE LAST TIME! I DIDN'T KNOW HE WAS OUR GRANDFATHER!

ELLI WANTS TO MAKE KISSES WITH FARFAR!

*SEE THOR: GOD OF THUNDER, GODBOMB TPB. --WIL

HOW WOULD YOU LIKE TO MAKE KISSES WITH MY MACE, ATLI?!

AND HOW ARE YOU AT REGROWING ARMS, SISTER?!

STOP IT, THE BOTH OF YOU. DAMMIT, GIVE ME THE DIAMOND...

TAKE US TO THOR!

RRRRGGGH!

STUPID! BLASTED! HAMMER!

STILL CAN... BARELY LIFT IT! GARRRRGGH!!!

GAAGGGGH!!! DEATH TO ALL HAMMERS!!!

DIDN'T EVEN GET TO SAVE THAT VIKING VILLAGE FROM TROLLS! SOMEONE ELSE HAD ALREADY THRASHED THEM!

HOW IN THE NAME OF THE GODS AM I SUPPOSED TO BECOME WORTHY OF THIS WRETCHED THING?!

SHOULD WE JUST TELL HIM HOW HE ENDS UP BECOMING WORTHY? IT CERTAINLY WASN'T FROM BATTLING TROLLS.

NO, HE'LL HAVE TO FIGURE THAT OUT FOR HIMSELF.

ALL RIGHT, DIAMOND, LET'S GET IT RIGHT THIS TIME. TAKE US TO SEE...THE FUTURE THOR!

no!

ELLISIV, WE HAVE TO GO BACK! WE HAVE TO STOP LOKI!

WE CAN'T INTERFERE IN OUR OWN FUTURE, FRIGG, NOT WITHOUT POTENTIALLY DESTROYING THE ENTIRE UNIVERSE!

WHERE THE HEL ARE WE *NOW?* LOOKS LIKE ANOTHER DUMP.

THIS ENTIRE TRIP WAS A MISTAKE. I NEVER SHOULD'VE LET YOU TWO TALK ME INTO THIS!

WHAT ARE YOU LOOKING AT, CAVEMAN?

WE ALL AGREED ON THIS! WE ALL WANTED TO SEE--

UGH.

OH, SORRY. I WASN'T WATCHING WHERE I WAS...

UMM... SHOULD I KNOW YOU GIRLS FROM SOMEWHERE?

IT'S HER.

IT'S YOU. YOU'RE...

JANE FOSTER.

YOU'RE THE THOR WE CAME TO SEE!

UH, OKAY. WELL, THEN I'M AFRAID I'VE GOT SOME BAD NEWS FOR YOU, LADIES.

I'M NOT THOR ANYMORE.

...AND I KNEW HE WOULD JUST KEEP COMING, NO MATTER WHAT. I KNEW THERE WAS NO OTHER WAY TO STOP HIM AND SAVE THE GODS.

SO I WRAPPED THE *MANGOG* IN CHAINS OF URU, FASTENED THEM TO MY HAMMER, AND I--

AND YOU THREW MJOLNIR INTO THE SUN. BELIEVE ME, WE ALL KNOW THE STORY BY HEART.

WE MADE GRANDFATHER TELL IT TO US ABOUT A MILLION TIMES!

ONCE WE FOUND THE BOOK, AT LEAST--THE OLD HISTORY BOOK IN THE ASGARDIAN LIBRARY THAT TOLD US ALL ABOUT YOU.

BEFORE THAT, HE NEVER LIKED TO TALK MUCH ABOUT THE OLD DAYS.

THE OLD DAYS, *HUH?* WHERE EXACTLY ARE YOU YOUNG LADIES FROM?

THE FUTURE!

THE FAR FUTURE.

THE *VERY* FAR FUTURE.

WE'RE THE *GRANDDAUGHTERS* OF KING THOR. WE'RE THE GODDESSES OF THUNDER.

AND WE'RE *HUGE* FANS, LADY JANE.

WELL, THEN I'M SORRY YOU CAME ALL THIS WAY JUST TO MEET A SHRIVELED-UP SHELL OF A WOMAN.

NO MORE HAMMER-SLINGING. NO MORE EPIC ADVENTURES FOR ME.

INSTEAD I'VE BEEN CIRCLING THIS BLOCK FOR AN HOUR, TOO SCARED TO GO INSIDE.

McCARTHY MEDICAL INSTITUTE

MARIA WHEELOCK CANCER CENTER

YOU WILL.

YOU'LL GO INSIDE AND FIGHT THIS BATTLE THE SAME WAY YOU FOUGHT THE MANGOG.

HAMMERS DON'T MAKE THE HERO. NOW *AXES*, ON THE OTHER HAND...

NO, LADY JANE, I DON'T BELIEVE WE CAME BACK TO THE WRONG TIME AT ALL.

I THINK YOU'RE *EXACTLY* THE WOMAN WE WANTED TO MEET.

THANK YOU, LADIES.

THANK *YOU*. WE LEARNED HOW TO BE GODDESSES OF THUNDER BY READING ABOUT YOU.

IS IT TRUE YOU PUNCHED ODIN THROUGH THREE PLANETS WHEN YOU GUYS FOUGHT?

IS IT TRUE WHAT THEY SAY YOU DID TO THE KING OF THE FROST GIANTS?

SHHH, SHE HASN'T DONE THAT YET.

I DON'T WANNA KNOW ABOUT THE FUTURE, GIRLS.

I'VE GOT MY HANDS FULL WITH *TODAY*.

BUT BEFORE I TAKE THIS NEXT STEP, HOW ABOUT YOU THUNDER GODDESSES DO ME JUST *ONE* LITTLE FAVOR?

SHE STILL HAD THE *THUNDER* IN HER VEINS. COULD YOU HEAR IT?

I CAN *STILL* HEAR IT.

I THINK THAT'S GRANDFATHER SNORING.

SHE WAS EVERYTHING I EXPECTED AND MORE.

SIGH I MISS HER ALREADY.

I MISS THE TROLLS.

I JUST WISH WE COULD'VE *TOLD* HER. ABOUT WHAT'S COMING. ABOUT THE *WAR OF THE REALMS.*

YOU KNOW WE COULDN'T. ESPECIALLY GIVEN THE ROLE SHE'LL PLAY IN IT. NO, I'M AFRAID JANE FOSTER WILL HAVE TO LEARN JUST LIKE EVERYONE ELSE...

MOTHER OF MAGGOTS SAVE US.

H-H-HERE, MY LORD.

AH YES, OF COURSE. WHAT A FINE-LOOKING LOT YOU ARE.

GREETINGS, FANGROTS! I BRING HAPPY NEWS OF YOUR ELDEST SON!

MY FIRSTBORN? HE'S ALIVE?

OH NO, HE'S QUITE DEAD. HE WAS KILLED RATHER GRUESOMELY JUST YESTERDAY IN NIDAVELLIR.

I SEE. A THOUSAND CURSES UPON THOSE WRETCHED DWARVES.

ACTUALLY, IT WASN'T WHO KILLED HIM.

HE WAS INDEED FIGHTING DWARVES, MOST FEROCIOUSLY FROM ALL ACCOUNTS. IN FACT, HE RUTHLESSLY BUTCHERED SO MANY THAT YOUR SON BECAME MURDER-CRAZED. BLOOD-DRUNK!

TO THE POINT WHERE EVEN AFTER EVERY DWARF IN THE VICINITY HAD BEEN THOROUGHLY EVISCERATED, YOUR BLESSED BOY WAS STILL SO CONSUMED WITH WARRIOR MADNESS THAT HE TURNED UPON HIS FELLOW DARK ELF TROOPS.

HE HAD TO BE PUT DOWN LIKE A RABID DOG, BY HIS OWN BROTHERS!

HA! ISN'T IT WONDERFUL? WHY, IF I HAD A THOUSAND SUCH KILLING MACHINES, THIS WAR WOULD BE WON ALREADY!

DOESN'T IT MAKE YOU BEAM WITH PRIDE, MOTHER FANGROT?

YES, MY LORD, I DEFINITELY FIND MYSELF OVERCOME...

...WITH PRIDE.

THEN TELL ME, MY DEAR LADY, WHAT BOON CAN YOUR KING GRANT YOU, IN THE NAME OF YOUR GLORIOUSLY BLOODTHIRSTY SON?

AND THIS... THIS IS THE MAGNIFICENT CREATION THAT MAKES IT ALL POSSIBLE.

MY PORTAL TO THE REALMS. MY *BLACK BIFROST.*

AS POWERFUL A TESTAMENT TO DARK ELF INGENUITY AS ONE WILL EVER SEE.

AND TO *LOKI*, THE GOD OF LIES, AS WELL.

AFTER ALL, WAS *HE* WHO GAVE YOU THE SECRETS OF THE ASGARDIAN *RAINBOW BRIDGE.*

AND 'TWAS *MALEKITH* WHO RESCUED *YOU* FROM THE SPIDERS OF HEL.

YOU'D DO WELL TO REMEMBER THAT, MY LADY, BEFORE NEXT YOU CHOOSE TO SPEAK.

YES, MY KING.

STAY HERE AND GUARD THE BIFROST FOR ME. AS USUAL, YOUR KING WILL ENJOY THE REST OF HIS MORNING STROLL...IN PEACE!

"ASGARD IS NO MORE."

DAYS EARLIER.
ASGARDIA.
HOME OF THE GODS.

KKRRRRRADDDOOOOOOOOOOOOOOOMMM

NO! THIS CAN'T BE HOW IT ENDS! HEALERS!

WHERE ARE THE BOR-DAMNED HEALERS?!

HEH. MY ONLY REGRET, SWEET LADY...

...IS THAT *I* WASN'T THE ONE TO KILL YOU.

DO ENJOY *VALHALLA*, MY DEAR.

FOR A MOMENT, AT LEAST.

FOR SOON I'LL BE BURNING *THAT* AS WELL.

MORTALS ARE SUCH... *FASCINATING* CREATURES, ARE THEY NOT?

COMPARED TO THE REST OF THE ANCIENT INHABITANTS OF THE TEN REALMS, MORTALS ARE NOTHING MORE THAN...

...WEAK LITTLE INFANTS WALLOWING IN THEIR OWN EXCREMENT.

YET SOMEHOW... THEY'RE STILL *ARROGANT* ENOUGH TO BELIEVE THAT THIS ALL REVOLVES AROUND THEM.

OH, JANE. YOU SHOULD'VE STAYED *DEAD*, YOU SILLY GIRL.

NOW YOU'LL HAVE TO WATCH AS ALL THIS BURNS AROUND YOU.

THESE MORTALS LIKE TO THINK THEY ARE THE CENTER OF ALL THE REALMS?

HEH. THEN SO BE IT.

This is the first drawing I did of Jane: a layout for what was originally just a variant cover. I never thought that nearly four years after drawing this, I'd be sitting here in a Jane Thor T-shirt, with a Jane Thor Funko figure on my desk, writing a letter to commemorate the last issue of Jane's long-running series.

That variant cover turned into the main cover and a new job for me. I thought the book would be a good fit (I love fantasy and mythology, billowing capes and flowing hair!), but I was still pretty nervous. I'd just started working for Marvel a few months before, I'd just gotten married — there was a lot of new going on. Plus, Jason's GOD OF THUNDER was one of my favorite comics, and following Esad's art had me intimidated. I wondered if our book would be as good, if it would sell, if anyone would care about this new Thor. And then I see Whoopi Goldberg pointing to my art on *The View*. And then Thor's identity is revealed and I start getting messages from readers saying how much Jane means to them.

I saved a screengrab of Whoopi pointing to the issue #1 cover. In the same folder, I've saved your messages. Thank you for sharing your stories about how you relate to Jane's struggle, or just for writing to say how much you like the book. I know we put you through the emotional wringer with this arc (sorry!), but I hope we did right by you with the finale. I hope we did Jane justice.

This is my last THOR issue, and I'll miss drawing Jane. But I'm thrilled that she has a complete story told by the same creative team (with some fantastic guests). I'm incredibly proud of the work everyone's done. Thank you to Jason for the brilliant ideas, amazing writing and thoughtful scripts, to Matt for the smart and unbelievably gorgeous colors, to Joe for stylishly making everything flow together, to Sarah (and past editors Jon Moisan, Charles Beacham and Chris Robinson!) for steering the ship so well, and to Wil for the guidance, thoughtfulness and opportunity.

I really lucked out, getting to work with some of the absolute best. Here's hoping that down the line, the rainbow bridge gets fixed and we all get teleported back to Asgard together.

In the meantime, I'm excited to see where Jason takes his amazing Thor saga, and I'm sure I'll be drooling over Mike del Mundo's art for it. I have more with Marvel in the pipeline, and I'll share as soon as I can.

Drawing THOR became an absolute dream project, one that will always mean the world to me. Thank you all so much for supporting Jane (and me, and the whole team)!

KRAKKAKOOOOM!
Russell

I never expected all this.

Before Jane became Thor, I'd never had fans come up to me in tears at signings, relating stories of their loved ones who'd passed or of their own battles with cancer.

Before Jane, I'd never had so many people screaming at me on Twitter, so enraged, oftentimes over a book they hadn't even read.

I'd never had a character I helped shape explode so epically, becoming toys and statues and cosplay at every con I've attended since.

Before Jane, I'd never cried while writing a script.

I've never been as emotionally invested in a super hero as I've been in her. And I've never felt such a profound emotional response from the fans as what Jane has generated.

I never imagined she'd become this important to so many people, including myself.

It all started when then-EIC Axel Alonso called and offered me the chance to relaunch THOR after my GOD OF THUNDER run. We agreed that it'd be a great opportunity to have someone else carry the mantle. Since I first took over the character, I knew at some point I wanted to do a Beta Ray Bill sorta story, where Thor's hammer would change hands. And for a while I'd had a vague idea about it being Thor's stepmom Freyja who'd eventually wield Mjolnir.

But as soon as we talked about the relaunch, I knew it had to be Jane.

I'd already shown that Jane was dealing with breast cancer. And as soon as I imagined her becoming Thor, the entire story clicked into place, right up through these last few issues, in a way that stories don't often do, not for me at least, not without a lot of pushing and pulling.

For years, I both eagerly awaited and thoroughly dreaded having to write this "Death of Thor" story. And for the last few months, I've felt the same way every single time I'd get a new email from Russell.

Not enough can be said about what Russell Dauterman and Matthew Wilson have accomplished together on this series. They have brought Jane to life and made her entire world sing and explode and burn in ways that should be remembered and studied and idolized for many eons to come. I cannot possibly thank them enough for all their amazing work, but I'll gladly spend the rest of my mortal life attempting to do so. In other words, the drinks are always on me, boys.

And those thanks and free drinks also go out to everyone else who's worked on the series, including letterer Joe Sabino and all the stellar guest artists, cover artists and assistant editors along the way. And even bigger thanks to editor Wil Moss, who has some of the best artistic tastes and creative instincts of any editor I've ever known. Another round of mead for all of you!

But most especially, thanks to you, the readers. For embracing Jane the way you have. For making her so much a part of your own lives. For making this entire run one of the most rewarding creative and emotional experiences of my entire life.

I'll never forget this Thor. And I'll never forget all of you. And I hope we'll all see each other again, in some other thunderous stories down the road.

Stay worthy.
Jason Aaron
KC, March 2018

RUSSELL DAUTERMAN CREATED A HEIGHT CHART WITH ALL OF HIS CHARACTER MODELS TO KEEP TRACK OF THEIR RELATIVE SIZES, ADDING CHARACTERS AS THE SERIES WENT ALONG. THIS IS THE RESULTING IMAGE!

THE DEATH OF
THE MIGHTY
THOR

by AARON, DAUTERMAN & WILSON

MIGHTY THOR #700 HOMAGE VARIANT
BY **STEPHANIE HANS**

MIGHTY THOR #700 VARIANT
BY **ADAM HUGHES**

THE MIGHTY THOR

HOW TO DRAW MJOLNIR
IN SIX EASY STEPS!
BY CHIP "WORTHLESS" ZDARSKY

Wow! A "sketch variant cover"! Studies show that drawing
keeps you mentally acute and generally unpopular!
Anyway, here's a fun and informative step-by-step guide!

1

2

3

First step: make a rectangle!
Easy, right? Roughly twice as
long as it is tall!

Now, even though we didn't
draw the rectangle in
perspective, we'll do a slight
cheat here, and draw its
bevels slightly slanted
downward!

Now, copy the entire bottom
line just underneath, but
make it a little smaller for
receding perspective. Then
connect the points!

4

5

6

Place a cylinder, like a paper
towel roll, below the
hammer's head, and then
show the hints of a larger disc
above! A center guide line will
help you place these!

Add a loose strap at the base and
wrap the handle in leather! Then, add
some shading and little details for the
stone and handle! I forget the quote
that's on the hammer, but it's
something like this. Basically to lift it
you have to be worthy, like, SUPER
worthy, or it will NOT budge. Done!

Now, protect your comic by
picking it up and placing it in
a bag and—oh.

Uh.

MIGHTY THOR #700 HOW TO DRAW VARIANT
BY **CHIP ZDARSKY**

MIGHTY THOR #700 1965 T-SHIRT VARIANT
BY **JACK KIRBY & DICK AYERS**

MIGHTY THOR #700 LEGACY HEADSHOT VARIANT
BY **MIKE McKONE & RACHELLE ROSENBERG**

MIGHTY THOR #700 MOVIE VARIANT

MIGHTY THOR #700 TRADING CARD VARIANT
BY **JOHN TYLER CHRISTOPHER**

MIGHTY THOR #701 VARIANT
BY **ALEX ROSS**

MIGHTY THOR #700 MOVIE VARIANT
BY **JACKSON SZE**

MIGHTY THOR #702 PHOENIX VARIANT
BY **KRIS ANKA**

MIGHTY THOR #704 HEROES REBORN VARIANT
BY **ROB LIEFELD & LEO PACIAROTTI**

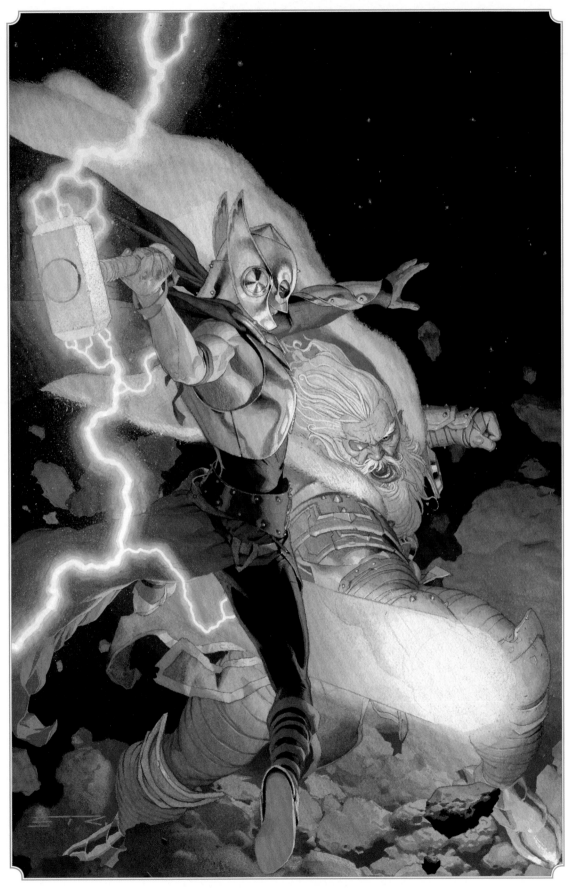

MIGHTY THOR #705 VARIANT
BY **ESAD RIBIĆ**

MIGHTY THOR #705 VARIANT
BY **ARTGERM**

MIGHTY THOR #705 VARIANT
BY **JEE-HYUNG LEE**

MIGHTY THOR #706 VARIANT
BY **WALTER SIMONSON** & **LAURA MARTIN**

MIGHTY THOR #706 VARIANT
BY **MARCO CHECCHETTO**

MIGHTY THOR: AT THE GATES OF VALHALLA VARIANT
BY **RON GARNEY & MATT MILLA**